Preface

The microchip industry is at the heart of modern technology, driving innovation and progress in countless fields. As the global demand for these tiny yet powerful devices continue to grow, India finds itself at a pivotal moment. With a burgeoning tech sector and increasing government support, the country is poised to become a significant player in the global microchip manufacturing landscape.

"Chip India: The Rise of Microchip Manufacturing in India" aims to provide a comprehensive overview of India's journey in this critical industry. This book explores the early beginnings, challenges, and milestones that have shaped India's microchip manufacturing capabilities. It also delves into current market dynamics, success stories, and the potential future of the industry.

The motivation behind this book stems from a desire to highlight India's emerging role in the global technology ecosystem. By chronicling the country's efforts and achievements, we hope to inspire further growth and investment in this sector. This book is intended for industry professionals, policymakers, students, and anyone interested in understanding the complexities and opportunities within the microchip manufacturing industry.

We express our gratitude to the numerous experts, industry veterans, and policymakers who provided invaluable insights and data for this book. Their contributions have been instrumental in creating a detailed and accurate narrative of India's microchip manufacturing journey.

[Dr. Jiteshwar Kumar Pandey]

M.A, Ph.D

Former Assistant Registrar Administration

NIFTEM

Comes Under Ministry of Food Processing Industries,

Government of India. 01 Aug 2024

Table of Contents

Introduction — Page No.

Overview of the Global Microchip Industry — 4-5

Importance of Microchip Manufacturing for India's Economic Growth — 6-10

Part I: Understanding Microchips

Chapter 1: What are Microchips? — 11-12

1.1: Definition and Types of Microchips — 13-14

1.2: Applications and Uses of Microchips — 15-16

Chapter 2: The Global Microchip Industry — 17-19

2.1: Market Size and Growth — 20-22

2.2: Key Players and Market Share — 23-25

2.3: Geopolitical Dynamics and Supply Chain Challenges — 26-28

Part II: India's Microchip Manufacturing Journey

Chapter 3: Early Beginnings — 29

3.1: India's First Microchip Manufacturing Unit — 30

3.2: Challenges and Limitations — 31-32

Chapter 4: Government Initiatives and Policies — 33-35

4.1: Government Support and Incentives — 36-37

4.2: Impact on the Industry — 38-39

Part III: Current Landscape

Chapter 5: Indian Microchip Manufacturing Industry — 40-42

5.1: Current Market Size and Growth — 43

5.2: Key Players and Market Share — 44-46

Chapter 6: Challenges and Opportunities — 47-49

6.1: Infrastructure and Talent Challenges — 50-51

6.2: Emerging Opportunities and Trends — 52-54

Part IV: Success Stories and Case Studies

Chapter 7: Existing Microchip Manufacturing Units

7.1: Profiles of Successful Units	55-56
7.2: Lessons Learned and Best Practices	57-58

Chapter 8: Startups and Innovators

8.1: Emerging Startups and Innovators	59
8.2: Impact on the Industry	60-61

Part V: Future Prospects

Chapter 9: Emerging Trends and Technologies — 62-64

9.1: Artificial Intelligence and Machine Learning	65-66
9.2: Internet of Things (IoT) and 5G	67
9.3: Quantum Computing and Advanced Materials	

Chapter 10: India's Potential for Global Leadership — 68

10.1: Opportunities for Growth and Expansion	69
10.2: Strategies for Success	70

Conclusion

Summary of Key Points

Call to Action for India's Microchip Manufacturing Industry

Appendices

Appendix A: Glossary of Microchip-Related Terms	71-72
Appendix B: List of Microchip Manufacturing Units in India	73-74
Appendix C: Timeline of Key Events in India's Microchip Industry	75

"Chip India: The Rise of Microchip Manufacturing in India"

Introduction

The Global Importance of Microchips

Microchips, also known as semiconductors or integrated circuits (ICs), are the foundational technology behind the digital age. They power everything from smartphones and computers to automobiles and industrial machinery. As the world increasingly depends on digital technology, the demand for advanced microchips has surged, making the semiconductor industry a critical component of the global economy.

The Global Semiconductor Landscape

Historically, the global semiconductor industry has been dominated by a few key regions, particularly the United States, South Korea, Taiwan, and Japan. These countries have developed extensive infrastructure, skilled workforces, and strong research and development (R&D) capabilities that have allowed them to lead in the design, production, and innovation of microchips. The strategic importance of this industry has become even more apparent in recent years, especially during geopolitical tensions and the COVID-19 pandemic, which exposed vulnerabilities in global supply chains.

India's Technological Aspirations

India, known for its robust IT services sector and a rapidly growing economy, has long aspired to establish itself as a significant player in the global technology landscape. However, the country has historically lagged in semiconductor manufacturing, relying heavily on imports to meet its domestic demand. Recognizing the strategic importance of self-reliance in this critical industry, the Indian government has launched numerous initiatives aimed at developing a domestic semiconductor ecosystem.

The Genesis of Microchip Manufacturing in India

The journey of microchip manufacturing in India can be traced back to the early 21st century, with sporadic attempts at establishing semiconductor fabrication plants, commonly known as fabs. However, these efforts faced numerous challenges, including high capital costs, insufficient infrastructure, and a lack of skilled manpower. Despite these obstacles, the vision of a self-reliant semiconductor industry persisted, driven by the need to support India's burgeoning electronics and information technology sectors.

Recent Developments and Government Initiatives

In the last decade, there has been a renewed focus on building a comprehensive semiconductor ecosystem in India. The government has announced several policy measures, including financial incentives, to attract investment in semiconductor manufacturing. Initiatives like the "Make in India" campaign and the "Atmanirbhar Bharat" (Self-Reliant India) mission have emphasized the importance of developing domestic capabilities in high-tech manufacturing sectors, including semiconductors.

In 2021, the Indian government launched the Production Linked Incentive (PLI) scheme for the electronics and semiconductor industries, aiming to boost local production and attract global players. This scheme, along with other measures such as the establishment of semiconductor research and development centres, has started to create a more conducive environment for the growth of the industry.

Strategic Importance and Future Prospects

The strategic importance of a robust semiconductor manufacturing capability cannot be overstated. It not only ensures supply chain security and reduces dependency on foreign suppliers but also positions India as a significant player in the global technology arena. With the advent of technologies such as 5G, artificial intelligence, and the Internet of Things (IoT), the demand for advanced semiconductors is set to grow exponentially. India's efforts to develop a strong semiconductor industry are crucial for leveraging these emerging technologies and achieving broader economic and technological goals.

Aim of this Book

This book, "The Rise of Microchip Manufacturing in India," aims to provide a comprehensive overview of the country's journey toward establishing a domestic semiconductor industry. The following chapters will explore the historical context, government policies, key players, challenges, and future prospects of microchip manufacturing in India. By examining the successes and setbacks along the way, the book seeks to offer insights into the opportunities and challenges that lie ahead for India in this strategically vital sector.

Importance of Microchip Manufacturing for India's Growth

Economic Growth and Employment

Microchip manufacturing, also known as semiconductor fabrication, is crucial for economic growth and job creation. The semiconductor industry is a cornerstone of modern technology, powering everything from smartphones to automobiles. Establishing a robust microchip manufacturing sector in India would not only reduce dependence on imports but also create high-value jobs in engineering, research, and skilled labour. This can contribute to GDP growth and help India climb the value chain in the global technology market.

Boost to the Electronics and IT Industry

India's electronics and IT sectors are among the fastest-growing in the world. However, the lack of a domestic semiconductor industry forces companies to rely on imported chips, which can be costly and vulnerable to supply chain disruptions. Developing indigenous chip manufacturing capabilities would bolster India's electronics industry, making it more competitive globally and fostering innovation in products like smartphones, computers, and medical devices.

Strategic Significance for Technology Independence

National Security and Self-Reliance

Microchips are fundamental to a wide range of critical technologies, including telecommunications, defense systems, and infrastructure. Dependency on foreign suppliers for these components can pose significant risks to national security. By building domestic semiconductor manufacturing capabilities, India can ensure the integrity and security of its critical infrastructure and reduce vulnerabilities associated with geopolitical tensions.

Sovereignty in Digital Infrastructure

As India moves towards greater digitization, the importance of having control over digital infrastructure cannot be overstated. Microchips are at the heart of data centres, telecommunications networks, and other critical digital infrastructure. By manufacturing its own chips, India can maintain greater sovereignty over its digital infrastructure, protecting against potential cyber threats and ensuring data privacy for its citizens.

Support for Emerging Technologies

Emerging technologies such as artificial intelligence (AI), 5G, the Internet of Things (IoT), and quantum computing rely heavily on advanced semiconductors. India's ambition to become a global leader in these fields necessitates a strong domestic semiconductor industry. Local manufacturing can accelerate the development and deployment of these technologies, fostering innovation and maintaining competitiveness in the global technology landscape.

Government Initiatives and Challenges

Policy Support and Incentives

Recognizing the strategic importance of semiconductors, the Indian government has launched initiatives like the Production Linked Incentive (PLI) scheme to attract investments in semiconductor manufacturing. These initiatives aim to create a favourable ecosystem by providing financial incentives, fostering research and development, and developing a skilled workforce.

Infrastructure and Resource Challenges

Building a semiconductor industry from scratch requires significant investment in infrastructure, such as fabs (fabrication plants), cleanrooms, and specialized equipment. Additionally, the industry demands a substantial supply of water and electricity, as well as access to rare materials. Addressing these challenges requires coordinated efforts between the government, private sector, and academia.

Conclusion

The development of a domestic microchip manufacturing industry is critical for India's economic growth, technological advancement, and strategic independence. By investing in this sector, India can secure its position in the global technology arena, protect its national security, and pave the way for future innovations. The road ahead is challenging but essential for building a self-reliant and resilient technological foundation.

Potential for Job Creation and Economic Development through Microchip Manufacturing in India

1. Direct Employment in Manufacturing and Engineering

Microchip manufacturing, or semiconductor fabrication, requires a diverse range of skills and expertise. The industry offers various job opportunities, including:

Skilled Labor and Technicians: Semiconductor fabs require a substantial number of technicians to operate and maintain complex machinery. These roles often demand specialized training in electronics, mechanics, and semiconductor processes.

Engineers: Design and process engineers play a crucial role in developing and optimizing semiconductor devices. This includes roles in electrical engineering, chemical engineering, materials science, and software engineering, particularly in the areas of chip design and testing.

Research and Development (R&D): R&D is a critical component of the semiconductor industry, driving innovation in chip design, materials, and manufacturing techniques. This sector can employ scientists and engineers focusing on cutting-edge technologies and process improvements.

2. Indirect Employment and Industry Spillover Effects

The establishment of a semiconductor manufacturing industry can spur job creation beyond the immediate sector through several channels:

Supply Chain Development: A robust semiconductor industry requires a complex supply chain, including raw materials, chemicals, manufacturing equipment, and logistics. Each of these areas creates additional employment opportunities.

Support Services: Industries such as IT services, legal, marketing, finance, and facility management will see increased demand as they support the semiconductor companies. This further broadens the employment base.

Related Industries: Industries that consume semiconductors, such as consumer electronics, automotive, telecommunications, and healthcare, will benefit from improved supply reliability and potentially lower costs. This can lead to expansion and further job creation in these sectors.

3. Economic Development and GDP Growth

The semiconductor industry has a significant multiplier effect on the economy due to its capital-intensive nature and high value-added activities. Key aspects include:

Attracting Foreign Investment: Establishing a semiconductor manufacturing ecosystem can attract significant foreign direct investment (FDI). This not only brings in capital but also facilitates technology transfer and enhances domestic technological capabilities.

Boosting Exports: With a competitive semiconductor manufacturing industry, India can increase its exports of chips and related products. Given the global demand for semiconductors, this presents a substantial opportunity for improving trade balances and generating foreign exchange.

Innovation and Competitiveness: A local semiconductor industry can foster innovation, not only in chip design but also in related technologies like AI, IoT, and advanced manufacturing. This can enhance the overall competitiveness of India's technology sector on a global scale.

4. Regional Economic Development

The establishment of semiconductor manufacturing hubs can lead to the economic revitalization of regions:

Infrastructure Development: Semiconductor fabs require high-quality infrastructure, including roads, electricity, water supply, and cleanrooms. Investments in these areas can benefit the broader community by improving overall infrastructure and quality of life.

Skill Development and Education: The demand for a skilled workforce can stimulate the growth of educational and vocational training institutions, leading to broader educational advancements and opportunities for the local population.

Urbanization and Real Estate: As semiconductor manufacturing hubs develop, they can spur urbanization, leading to the growth of cities and towns. This can boost the real estate market and create jobs in construction and services.

5. Challenges and Considerations

While the potential for job creation and economic development is substantial, several challenges need to be addressed:

Capital Investment: Semiconductor manufacturing is highly capital-intensive, requiring significant upfront investment in facilities and technology.

Skilled Workforce: There is a need to develop a skilled workforce through education and training programs tailored to the needs of the semiconductor industry.

Sustainable Practices: Given the industry's high water and energy consumption, sustainable practices and resource management are crucial for long-term viability.

Conclusion

Investing in microchip manufacturing presents a transformative opportunity for job creation and economic development in India. It can catalyse growth in various sectors, enhance technological capabilities, and position India as a significant player in the global technology landscape. Addressing the associated challenges will require coordinated efforts from the government, industry, and educational institutions to ensure sustainable and inclusive growth.

Chapter: 01

What are Microchips

Microchips, also known as integrated circuits (ICs), are small electronic devices made up of a set of interconnected electronic components, such as transistors, resistors, and capacitors. These components are miniaturized and fabricated onto a small piece of semiconductor material, usually silicon. Microchips are the fundamental building blocks of modern electronic devices, including computers, smartphones, and various other digital and analog systems.

Here is a detailed breakdown of key aspects of microchips:

1. Structure and Fabrication

Substrate: The base material, typically silicon, upon which microchips are built. Silicon is preferred due to its excellent electrical properties and abundance.

Transistors: The primary building blocks of microchips, functioning as switches that can turn on or off to control the flow of electrical current. Microchips can contain billions of transistors.

Other Components: Resistors, capacitors, and other passive components are also integrated into the chip to manage and direct electrical currents.

Layers: Microchips are made of multiple layers. These layers include the substrate, various metal interconnections, and insulating layers, all precisely arranged to form a complete circuit.

Fabrication Process: The creation of microchips involves photolithography, where patterns are etched onto the silicon wafer using light. This process allows for the precise construction of circuits at microscopic scales.

2. Types of Microchips

Digital Microchips: These chips process binary data (0s and 1s) and are used in computers, smartphones, and digital devices. They include processors, memory chips, and logic chips.

Analog Microchips: These chips deal with continuous signals and are used in applications like audio and radio frequency processing.

Mixed-Signal Chips: Combine both analog and digital components, commonly used in devices like smartphones that handle both types of signals.

3. Applications

Computers and Smartphones: Microchips are crucial for processing data, memory storage, and managing various functionalities in computing devices.

Consumer Electronics: They are found in televisions, gaming consoles, cameras, and many other gadgets.

Automotive: Used in engine control units, infotainment systems, and advanced driver-assistance systems (ADAS).

Medical Devices: Essential for devices like pacemakers, imaging systems, and diagnostic tools.

Industrial and Military: Used in control systems, communication devices, and other specialized equipment.

4. Advancements and Trends

Miniaturization: The trend towards smaller, more powerful microchips continues, with advances in nanotechnology and fabrication techniques. Moore's Law, which predicts the doubling of transistors on a chip approximately every two years, has historically driven this trend.

Energy Efficiency: As devices become more compact, there is a growing emphasis on energy-efficient designs to reduce power consumption and heat generation.

Artificial Intelligence (AI) and Machine Learning: Specialized chips, such as GPUs (Graphics Processing Units) and TPUs (Tensor Processing Units), are being developed to handle the intensive computational tasks required for AI and machine learning applications.

5. Challenges

Fabrication Complexity: The process of manufacturing microchips is highly complex and expensive, requiring clean rooms and sophisticated equipment.

Supply Chain: The global supply chain for microchips is intricate

Definition and Types of Microchips: Microchips, also known as integrated circuits (ICs), are small electronic devices composed of interconnected components such as transistors, resistors, and capacitors. These components are miniaturized and fabricated onto a semiconductor material, typically silicon, to perform various electronic functions. Microchips are essential components in modern electronic devices, enabling data processing, storage, and communication.

Types of Microchips

Microchips can be categorized based on their functions and applications. Here are some of the primary types:

1. Digital Microchips

Microprocessors: The central processing unit (CPU) of a computer, responsible for executing instructions and managing the operations of other components.

Memory Chips: Store data and instructions. Types include RAM (Random Access Memory) for temporary data storage and ROM (Read-Only Memory) for permanent storage.

Logic Chips: Perform specific logical functions such as arithmetic operations, data handling, and control logic in digital circuits.

2. Analog Microchips

Operational Amplifiers (Op-Amps): Used to amplify voltage signals and perform mathematical operations in analog circuits.

Analog-to-Digital Converters (ADCs): Convert analog signals into digital data, essential in devices like digital cameras and audio recording equipment.

Digital-to-Analog Converters (DACs): Convert digital data back into analog signals, used in audio playback devices and signal processing systems.

3. Mixed-Signal Microchips

Microcontrollers: Combine a CPU with memory and input/output peripherals on a single chip. Used in embedded systems for controlling devices and processes.

System on Chip (SoC): Integrates all components of a computer or other electronic system into a single chip, including the CPU, memory, input/output ports, and sometimes, a GPU (Graphics Processing Unit). Common in smartphones and tablets.

4. Specialized Microchips

Graphics Processing Units (GPUs): Designed to handle complex graphics and image processing tasks, widely used in gaming, video editing, and AI applications.

Application-Specific Integrated Circuits (ASICs): Customized for a particular application or function, offering optimized performance for specific tasks.

5. Microcontrollers:

These are integrated systems containing a microprocessor, memory, and input/output peripherals on a single chip. They are used in embedded systems, such as automotive control systems, appliances, and IoT devices.

6. Memory Chips:

These are used to store data and include types like RAM (Random Access Memory), ROM (Read-Only Memory), Flash memory, and EEPROM (Electrically Erasable Programmable Read-Only Memory).

7. Application-Specific Integrated Circuits (ASICs):

These are custom-designed chips for specific applications or functions. They are used in a wide range of products, from consumer electronics to industrial equipment.

8. System on Chip (SoC):

This integrates all components of a computer or other electronic systems into a single chip, including the CPU, memory, and peripheral interfaces. SoCs are commonly used in smartphones and tablets.

Each type of microchip is designed for specific applications and has different characteristics in terms of power consumption, processing power, and integration level.

Applications and Uses of Microchips

Microchips are integral to modern technology, powering a vast array of devices and systems across various industries. Here are some key applications and uses of microchips:

1. Consumer Electronics

Smartphones and Tablets: Microchips such as processors, memory chips, and sensors are central to the functioning of these devices, enabling tasks from computing to connectivity.

Computers and Laptops: Microprocessors, memory, and graphic chips form the core components, driving both hardware and software operations.

Wearables: Smartwatches and fitness trackers use microchips for processing, data storage, and connectivity features.

2. Automotive Industry

Engine Control Units (ECUs): Microcontrollers in ECUs manage engine functions, improving efficiency and reducing emissions.

Infotainment Systems: Chips handle everything from audio and navigation to connectivity and user interfaces.

Advanced Driver-Assistance Systems (ADAS): Microchips enable features like lane departure warning, adaptive cruise control, and automatic braking.

3. Healthcare and Medical Devices

Diagnostic Equipment: Devices such as MRI machines, ultrasound scanners, and blood glucose meters rely on microchips for accurate data processing and analysis.

Wearable Health Devices: Microchips power wearable monitors that track vital signs and other health metrics, providing real-time data to users and healthcare professionals.

Implantable Devices: Pacemakers and insulin pumps use microchips for precise control and monitoring of medical conditions.

4. Industrial and Manufacturing

Automation Systems: Microcontrollers and programmable logic controllers (PLCs) are used in automated production lines, robotics, and control systems.

Sensors and Monitoring: Chips are used in various sensors to monitor environmental conditions, machinery performance, and other parameters.

Energy Management: Smart grid technology and renewable energy systems use microchips for efficient energy distribution and management.

5. Telecommunications

Network Infrastructure: Microchips are essential in routers, switches, and other networking equipment, enabling data transmission and communication.

5G Technology: The rollout of 5G networks relies on advanced microchips for faster data speeds and reduced latency.

6. Aerospace and Defense

Navigation and Control Systems: Aircraft and spacecraft use microchips in navigation, communication, and control systems.

Surveillance and Reconnaissance: Chips are used in various sensors and imaging devices for military and intelligence applications.

7. IoT (Internet of Things)

Smart Home Devices: Microchips power devices like smart thermostats, lighting systems, and security cameras, enabling automation and remote control.

Wearable Tech: IoT devices use microchips to connect and interact with other devices and the internet.

Industrial IoT: In manufacturing and logistics, microchips facilitate the monitoring and management of equipment, assets, and processes.

Chapter 2: The Global Microchip Industry

The global microchip industry is a dynamic and crucial sector within the technology landscape, driving advancements across various fields. Here's a detailed look at its structure, trends, and key players:

1. Industry Overview

Market Size and Growth: The global microchip industry is valued at several hundred billion dollars, with substantial growth projections driven by increasing demand in electronics, automotive, telecommunications, and other sectors. Market growth is influenced by the rising need for advanced computing power, the proliferation of IoT devices, and technological advancements like AI and 5G.

Types of Microchips:

Semiconductors: The foundational material for microchips, typically silicon, is used in various forms including ICs, transistors, and sensors.

Integrated Circuits (ICs): These are critical for processing and control functions in electronic devices.

Microprocessors: Serve as the central processing units in computers and many electronic devices.

Memory Chips: Include RAM, ROM, Flash, and other types of data storage solutions.

Sensors: Used in various applications from consumer electronics to industrial machinery.

2. Major Players

Semiconductor Manufacturers:

Intel Corporation: Leading in microprocessors and computing solutions, Intel is a key player in the consumer electronics and data centre markets.

Samsung Electronics: A major supplier of memory chips and processors, Samsung is influential in both consumer and industrial electronics.

Taiwan Semiconductor Manufacturing Company (TSMC): The world's largest contract semiconductor manufacturer, TSMC produces chips for numerous tech giants.

Qualcomm: Specializes in mobile processors and modem technology, crucial for smartphones and wireless communication.

NVIDIA: Known for its graphics processing units (GPUs) used in gaming, AI, and high-performance computing.

Equipment and Materials Suppliers: Companies like Applied Materials, ASML, and Lam Research provide the essential equipment and materials for chip fabrication.

3. Supply Chain and Manufacturing

Design and Development: Design Firms: Companies like ARM Holdings design semiconductor architectures used by various manufacturers.

Research and Development: Significant investments in R&D drive innovations in chip performance, size, and power efficiency.

Fabrication:

Foundries: Facilities where semiconductor fabrication occurs. TSMC, GlobalFoundries, and SMIC are notable examples.

Process Technology: Advances such as 5nm and 3nm process nodes improve chip performance and energy efficiency.

Assembly and Testing: Chips are assembled into packages and tested for functionality and reliability before they are shipped to customers.

4. Trends and Challenges

Technological Advancements:

Miniaturization: Continuous efforts to shrink chip sizes while increasing performance.

AI and Machine Learning: Chips optimized for AI tasks, such as NVIDIA's GPUs and specialized AI accelerators.

5G Technology: Development of chips to support high-speed, low-latency communication.

Supply Chain Issues:

Shortages: The industry has faced significant chip shortages due to supply chain disruptions, geopolitical tensions, and surging demand.

Geopolitical Risks: Trade policies, particularly between the U.S. and China, impact the global chip supply chain.

Sustainability and Environmental Impact:

The industry is addressing concerns about environmental impact by developing energy-efficient technologies and sustainable manufacturing practices.

5. Regional Dynamics

Asia-Pacific:

Dominates in manufacturing and assembly, with countries like Taiwan, South Korea, and China playing pivotal roles in the supply chain.

North America:

A hub for design and innovation, with key players based in the U.S. and significant influence in setting industry standards.

Europe: Focuses on high-end semiconductor technology and automotive applications, with companies like ASML leading in photolithography equipment. The global microchip industry is a cornerstone of modern technology, driving progress across multiple sectors and facing both opportunities and challenges as it evolves.

The market size and growth of the microchip industry reflect its critical role in modern technology and its broad applications across various sectors. Here's a detailed breakdown:

1. Market Size

Global Market Valuation: Current Market Size: As of 2024, the global semiconductor market is valued at approximately $600 billion to $700 billion. This includes microchips, integrated circuits (ICs), sensors, and related components.

Market Segmentation: The market is divided into several segments, including memory chips, microprocessors, analog ICs, and others. Each segment has its own growth trajectory based on demand and technological advancements.

Regional Market Size:

Asia-Pacific: This region holds the largest share of the semiconductor market, driven by major manufacturing hubs in countries like Taiwan, South Korea, and China. The region accounts for over 60% of global semiconductor production.

North America: Home to leading semiconductor design firms and technology companies, the U.S. has a significant market share, particularly in advanced chip design and R&D.

Europe: While smaller compared to Asia-Pacific and North America, Europe is notable for high-end semiconductor technology and applications, especially in automotive and industrial sectors.

2. Market Growth

Growth Rate:

Historical Growth: The semiconductor industry has experienced steady growth over the past few decades, with average annual growth rates of around 5-10%.

Projected Growth: The market is expected to grow at a compound annual growth rate (CAGR) of approximately 7-10% over the next several years. This growth is fueled by increasing demand for advanced electronics, automotive applications, and emerging technologies.

Key Drivers of Growth:

Technological Advancements: Innovations in chip technology, including smaller process nodes (e.g., 5nm, 3nm), improve performance and efficiency, driving demand for newer chips.

IoT Expansion: The proliferation of Internet of Things (IoT) devices contributes to growth, as microchips are essential for connecting and managing smart devices.

5G Deployment: The rollout of 5G networks requires advanced semiconductor solutions for faster data speeds and enhanced connectivity.

AI and Machine Learning: Increasing use of AI and machine learning technologies necessitates specialized chips such as GPUs and AI accelerators.

Automotive Electronics: The growth of electric vehicles (EVs) and advanced driver-assistance systems (ADAS) drives demand for automotive-grade semiconductors.

Market Trends:

Miniaturization: Continued push towards smaller, more powerful chips to meet the demands of mobile and consumer electronics.

Integration and System-on-Chip (SoC) Solutions: Rising use of SoCs to integrate multiple functions into a single chip, optimizing performance and reducing costs.

Sustainability: Growing focus on environmentally friendly manufacturing practices and energy-efficient technologies.

Challenges and Constraints:

Supply Chain Disruptions: Recent shortages and disruptions have impacted the semiconductor market, affecting production and delivery timelines.

Geopolitical Tensions: Trade conflicts, particularly between the U.S. and China, influence global supply chains and market dynamics.

High Capital Expenditure: The cost of developing and maintaining advanced semiconductor manufacturing facilities is substantial, posing financial challenges for companies.

3. Future Outlook

Emerging Applications:

Quantum Computing: Developing microchips for quantum computers could drive new growth opportunities in the coming years.

Advanced Robotics and Automation: Increasing use of robots in various sectors will require advanced semiconductor solutions.

Wearable Technology: Growth in health and fitness wearables will continue to drive demand for specialized chips.

Investment and Innovation:

Research and Development: Ongoing investment in R&D is crucial for maintaining competitiveness and addressing future technological needs.

Strategic Partnerships: Collaborations between semiconductor companies, tech firms, and governments are expected to shape the future landscape of the industry.

The microchip industry's market size and growth are influenced by a combination of technological innovation, expanding applications, and market dynamics. As technology advances and new applications emerge, the industry is poised for continued growth and evolution.

Key Players and Market Share: The microchip market is a critical sector within the global electronics industry, encompassing a wide range of companies that design and manufacture semiconductor devices. Here's an overview of the key players and their market share:

Key Players:

1. Intel Corporation:

Role: A leading manufacturer of microprocessors, which are central to computing devices such as PCs and servers.

Market Share: Historically holds a significant share in the microprocessor market. Intel's dominance has been challenged recently by AMD and other competitors.

2. Advanced Micro Devices (AMD):

Role: Known for its microprocessors and GPUs. AMD has gained market share with its Ryzen and EPYC processors, competing directly with Intel.

Market Share: Has been increasing, especially in the desktop and server markets.

3. NVIDIA Corporation:

Role: Primarily known for its GPUs, NVIDIA is also influential in AI and data center markets.

Market Share: Dominates the GPU market and has a growing presence in AI and deep learning applications.

4. Qualcomm Incorporated:

Role: A major player in the mobile chip market, particularly for its Snapdragon processors used in smartphones and tablets.

Market Share: Significant in the mobile and wireless sectors.

5. Samsung Electronics:

Role: A leading manufacturer of memory chips (DRAM and NAND) and system-on-chip (SoC) solutions.

Market Share: A dominant force in the memory chip market and a significant player in SoCs.

6. Texas Instruments (TI):

Role: Known for analog and embedded processing chips used in a wide range of applications.

Market Share: Strong presence in the analog chip market.

7. Broadcom Inc

Role: Supplies a broad range of semiconductor solutions including networking, broadband, and enterprise storage chips.

Market Share: Significant in the networking and broadband markets.

8. Micron Technology

Role: Major player in memory and storage solutions, particularly DRAM and NAND flash.

Market Share: Key competitor in the memory market.

9. Infineon Technologies

Role: Specializes in automotive, industrial, and security-related semiconductor solutions.

Market Share: Notable in the automotive and industrial sectors.

10. NXP Semiconductors

Role: Focuses on automotive, industrial, and IoT applications.

Market Share: Prominent in automotive and IoT markets.

Market Share Insights

Processors: Intel and AMD dominate the CPU market for PCs and servers, while NVIDIA leads in GPUs.

Memory: Samsung, Micron, and SK Hynix are the top players in the DRAM and NAND flash markets.

Mobile Chips: Qualcomm is a leader in mobile processors, while MediaTek also holds a significant share.

Automotive and Industrial: Infineon and NXP are key players.

The market share of these companies can vary based on technological advancements, shifts in consumer demand, and geopolitical factors. The semiconductor industry is also marked by consolidation and strategic partnerships, which can influence market dynamics.

Geopolitical Dynamics and Supply Chain Challenges: Geopolitical dynamics and supply chain challenges are closely interlinked and can have significant impacts on global trade, economics, and security. Here's a detailed overview:

Geopolitical Dynamics

1. Regional Conflicts and Tensions:

Trade Routes: Conflicts or tensions in key regions can disrupt major trade routes. For example, disputes in the South China Sea can impact maritime shipping routes.

Sanctions and Trade Barriers: Countries involved in geopolitical conflicts may face sanctions or trade restrictions, affecting global supply chains.

2. International Relations:

Alliances and Rivalries: Alliances (e.g., NATO) and rivalries (e.g., US-China tensions) can influence trade policies, military presence, and economic strategies, impacting global supply chains.

Diplomatic Relations: Diplomatic relations can affect trade agreements and collaborations. For instance, improved relations between countries can lead to more open trade policies, while strained relations can result in trade barriers.

3. National Security Policies:

Defense Priorities: National security policies can drive countries to prioritize self-sufficiency in critical industries, impacting global supply chains.

Cybersecurity: Geopolitical tensions often lead to increased focus on cybersecurity, as countries protect their digital infrastructure from potential threats.

4. Economic Policies

Tariffs and Trade Agreements: Geopolitical decisions often lead to changes in tariffs and trade agreements, affecting the cost and flow of goods.

Currency Fluctuations: Geopolitical events can cause currency volatility, impacting international trade and investment.

Supply Chain Challenges

1. Disruptions and Risks:

Natural Disasters and Pandemics: Events like earthquakes, hurricanes, or pandemics (e.g., COVID-19) can disrupt production and distribution networks.

Political Instability: Political unrest or changes in government can lead to unpredictable supply chain disruptions.

2. Globalization and Complexity:

Complex Networks: Global supply chains often involve multiple stakeholders across different countries, making them vulnerable to disruptions in any part of the chain.

Just-In-Time Inventory: Many companies use just-in-time inventory systems to minimize costs, which can be risky during disruptions.

3. Logistical and Transportation Issues:

Infrastructure: Poor infrastructure in some regions can lead to delays and increased costs in transportation and logistics.

Shipping Bottlenecks: Ports and shipping lanes can experience bottlenecks, affecting the timely delivery of goods.

4. Supply Chain Resilience:

Diversification: Companies are increasingly diversifying their supply sources to mitigate risks. This includes sourcing from multiple suppliers or regions.

Technology and Innovation: Advances in technology, such as blockchain and AI, are being used to enhance supply chain visibility and efficiency.

Interconnection Between Geopolitical Dynamics and Supply Chains

Strategic Resources: Geopolitical dynamics often centre around strategic resources (e.g., oil, rare earth metals). Disruptions in access to these resources can impact global supply chains.

Trade Policies: Changes in trade policies due to geopolitical shifts can alter supply chain strategies, such as reshoring or nearshoring production.

Security Measures: Geopolitical tensions can lead to increased security measures, affecting the movement of goods and people across borders.

Understanding these dynamics helps businesses and governments navigate the complexities of global trade and manage the risks associated with supply chain disruptions.

Chapter: 03

India's First Microchip Manufacturing Unit

India's journey into microchip manufacturing has evolved significantly over the decades. Here's a detailed look at its early beginnings and development:

Early Beginnings (1980s-1990s)

1. Initial Efforts

1984: The Indian government, recognizing the potential of electronics, established the Department of Electronics (DoE) to promote and develop the electronics industry. This included a focus on semiconductor technology.

1989: India launched the National Semiconductor Mission (NSM), which aimed to develop indigenous capabilities in semiconductor design and manufacturing. The mission was intended to reduce dependence on foreign technology and boost domestic production.

2. Early Investments

1990s: The Indian government started encouraging foreign investments and partnerships to gain technology and expertise in the semiconductor field. Companies like Intel and Texas Instruments set up research and development (R&D) centres in India during this period.

3. Policy Support

1996: The government announced the Electronics Policy, which included incentives for setting up semiconductor fabrication units. However, challenges like high costs and infrastructure issues hindered progress in establishing manufacturing plants.

Key Developments and Challenges (2000s)

1. Growth of the Design Industry: - By the early 2000s, India had become a significant player in semiconductor design. Companies like Wipro, Infosys, and Tata Consultancy

Services (TCS) began providing design services for global semiconductor firms. India established itself as a hub for electronic design automation (EDA) and intellectual property (IP) development.

2. Fabrication Challenges: - Despite success in design, India struggled with establishing its own semiconductor fabrication (fab) plants due to the high cost of technology, infrastructure challenges, and lack of advanced facilities. The focus remained on design and development rather than manufacturing.

3. Policy Revisions

2007: The Indian government introduced the National Policy on Electronics (NPE) with a focus on promoting the electronics industry, including semiconductor manufacturing. The policy aimed to create a conducive environment for electronics manufacturing by offering incentives and support.

Recent Developments (2010s-Present)

1. Attracting Investment

2010s: India started focusing on attracting investment in semiconductor manufacturing. The government proposed setting up semiconductor fabrication units and provided various incentives to foreign and domestic companies.

2. The Semiconductor Policy (2020)

2020: The Indian government unveiled a new semiconductor policy to boost domestic manufacturing. This policy includes incentives for setting up fabs, research, and development centres, and the development of a semiconductor ecosystem. The aim is to build a robust supply chain and reduce reliance on imports.

3. Initiatives and Partnerships

2021: The government announced significant initiatives to develop semiconductor manufacturing capabilities, including collaborations with global semiconductor giants and technology companies. India is also working on establishing semiconductor clusters to support the industry.

4. Recent Announcements

2022: The Indian government approved incentives for setting up semiconductor fabs, with several companies expressing interest in setting up production facilities in the country. India is aiming to build its own fabs to strengthen its position in the global semiconductor supply chain.

India's microchip manufacturing journey reflects a gradual but steady progression from initial efforts in the 1980s to a more focused and ambitious approach in recent years. The country is now working to leverage its strengths in design and technology to build a comprehensive semiconductor ecosystem.

India's efforts to establish its first microchip manufacturing unit have been a significant milestone in the country's journey toward becoming a major player in the semiconductor industry. Here's a detailed look at the key developments related to this endeavour:

Early Efforts and Challenges

1. Historical Context

1984: The Indian government launched the National Semiconductor Mission (NSM) to promote semiconductor technology, which included efforts to set up a domestic fabrication unit. However, the mission faced various challenges, including high costs, technological hurdles, and inadequate infrastructure.

2. Challenges in Setting Up a Fab: - Throughout the 1990s and early 2000s, India faced substantial challenges in setting up a semiconductor fab due to high capital expenditure, complex technology, and lack of specialized infrastructure. The focus was largely on semiconductor design and research rather than actual manufacturing.

The First Fab: ISMC (India Semiconductor Manufacturing Company)

1. ISMC Establishment

2006: - The India Semiconductor Manufacturing Company (ISMC) was established as the first major attempt to set up a semiconductor fab in India. The company was formed as a joint venture between the Indian private sector and foreign partners, aiming to build a semiconductor manufacturing facility in the country.

2. Location and Investment: - The proposed fab was planned to be located in Bangalore, Karnataka, a city already known for its strong IT and electronics industry. Initial investment plans included significant funding from various sources, including private equity and foreign investment.

3. Technical and Operational Details: - ISMC aimed to leverage advanced semiconductor manufacturing technology and build a state-of-the-art facility capable of producing various microchips. The goal was to create a competitive advantage for India in semiconductor manufacturing and reduce reliance on imports.

4. Challenges and Delays: - Despite initial enthusiasm, the project faced several challenges, including financial hurdles, regulatory issues, and technological complexities. These issues led to delays in the construction and operationalization of the fab. The project struggled to achieve its initial targets and faced difficulties in securing sustained investment.

Recent Developments and Future Prospects

1. Revival and New Initiatives: - In recent years, the Indian government has renewed its focus on semiconductor manufacturing with new policies and incentives. The National Semiconductor Policy introduced in 2020 and subsequent announcements have aimed to create a more favourable environment for semiconductor fabs.

2. New Investments: - As of 2023, India has attracted interest from several global semiconductor companies to set up manufacturing facilities. Initiatives include collaborations with major players and investments in infrastructure to support semiconductor production.

3. Future Goals: - India aims to establish multiple semiconductor fabs in the coming years, driven by government incentives and strategic partnerships. The focus is on creating a robust semiconductor ecosystem, including design, fabrication, and supply chain capabilities.

In summary, while ISMC was a pioneering effort in India's microchip manufacturing journey, it faced significant hurdles that impacted its success. However, recent policies and investments signal a renewed commitment to developing a comprehensive semiconductor manufacturing sector in India.

Chapter: 4

Government Initiatives and Policies

The Indian government has launched several initiatives and policies to boost the manufacturing of microchips and strengthen the domestic semiconductor industry. Here's a detailed overview of these efforts

1. National Semiconductor Mission (NSM)

Launched: 2007: - Objective: To promote the growth of the semiconductor industry in India by developing indigenous capabilities in semiconductor design, technology, and manufacturing.

Key Focus Areas: - The mission included establishing semiconductor fabrication units, developing intellectual property (IP), and creating a robust ecosystem for electronics and semiconductors.

2. National Policy on Electronics (NPE)

Introduced: 2012

Revised: 2019

Objective: To promote the growth of the electronics industry, including semiconductor manufacturing. It aims to reduce reliance on imports and encourage domestic production.

Key Features

Incentives: Financial incentives and subsidies for setting up semiconductor manufacturing units.

Infrastructure Support: Development of electronics clusters and parks to support manufacturing activities.

Skill Development: Programs to enhance skills and knowledge in electronics and semiconductor manufacturing.

3. Atmanirbhar Bharat (Self-Reliant India) Initiative

Launched: 2020

Objective: To enhance self-reliance in various sectors, including semiconductors. This initiative is part of a broader effort to boost domestic production and reduce dependence on imports.

Key Actions:

Production Linked Incentive (PLI) Scheme: The PLI scheme offers incentives to companies that invest in semiconductor manufacturing and related areas. It provides financial benefits based on the production volume and investment made in the sector.

Support for Startups and R&D: Encouragement for innovation and research in semiconductor technology through grants and funding.

4. Semiconductor Policy (2021)

Objective: To establish India as a global hub for semiconductor design and manufacturing.

Key Features:

Financial Support: Significant financial incentives for setting up semiconductor fabrication units (fabs), including subsidies and tax benefits.

Infrastructure Development: Plans to build semiconductor clusters and dedicated infrastructure to support the industry.

Public-Private Partnerships: Collaboration with international semiconductor companies to bring advanced technology and expertise to India.

Research and Development: Investment in R&D to foster innovation in semiconductor technology and related fields.

5. Electronics Manufacturing Clusters (EMCs)

Objective: To create dedicated zones for electronics manufacturing, including semiconductor fabrication.

Key Features:

Infrastructure Development: Development of specialized infrastructure and facilities to support electronics and semiconductor manufacturing.

Incentives: Financial incentives and support for companies setting up operations in these clusters.

6. National Electronics Policy (NEP)

Launched: 2020

Objective: To make India a global leader in electronics manufacturing, including semiconductors.

Key Components:

Investment Promotion: Incentives for domestic and international investments in electronics and semiconductor manufacturing.

Skill Development: Programs to enhance skills and knowledge in electronics and semiconductor technology.

7. Support for Research and Innovation

Objective: To advance semiconductor technology through research and innovation.

Key Initiatives:

Funding for R&D: Grants and funding for research projects related to semiconductor technology.

Collaboration with Academia: Partnerships between industry and academic institutions to drive innovation in semiconductor technology.

Summary

The Indian government's initiatives and policies aim to build a comprehensive semiconductor ecosystem by focusing on infrastructure development, financial incentives, public-private partnerships, and research and innovation. These efforts are designed to attract investments, enhance domestic manufacturing capabilities, and position India as a significant player in the global semiconductor market.

The Indian government has been actively working to promote the domestic manufacturing of microchips and semiconductor components as part of its broader strategy to bolster the country's electronics and technology sectors. Here's a detailed overview of the support and incentives provided:

1. Semiconductor Mission: - In December 2021, the Indian government launched the Semiconductor Mission under the Ministry of Electronics and Information Technology (MeitY). The mission aims to establish India as a global hub for semiconductor design, manufacturing, and research.

2. Production-Linked Incentive (PLI) Scheme

The government introduced the PLI Scheme for Semiconductors and Display Manufacturing to encourage investment in semiconductor manufacturing. Key aspects include:

Incentives: Financial incentives are provided based on incremental sales of manufactured goods. The scheme offers support for both setting up semiconductor fabs and display fabs.

Eligibility: Companies investing in semiconductor fabrication units, display fabrication units, and semiconductor assembly and testing are eligible.

Investment Support: It provides up to 50% of the project cost in the form of subsidies to eligible companies.

Support Duration: The PLI scheme extends over a period of 5 to 7 years, depending on the component.

3. National Policy on Electronics (NPE) 2019

The NPE 2019 outlines a framework to boost the electronics manufacturing ecosystem. Key points include:

Infrastructure Development: Setting up electronics manufacturing clusters with state-of-the-art infrastructure.

Financial Support: Grants and subsidies for setting up electronics manufacturing units and R&D centres.

Skill Development: Programs to train the workforce in electronics and semiconductor technologies.

4. Foreign Direct Investment (FDI) Policies

The Indian government has relaxed FDI norms to attract foreign investments in semiconductor manufacturing. This includes:

100% FDI: Automatic route for foreign investments in semiconductor and electronics sectors.

Tax Benefits: Exemptions and reductions in customs duties on imported components and machinery for semiconductor manufacturing.

5. Research and Development (R&D) Support

The government provides support for R&D through various programs:

Technology Development Fund (TDF): Provides financial assistance for developing advanced technologies, including semiconductor technologies.

Partnerships with Institutions: Collaborations with IITs, NITs, and other research institutions to advance semiconductor technology and innovation.

6. Infrastructure Development

Electronics Manufacturing Clusters (EMCs): Establishment of EMCs across India to provide world-class infrastructure, including logistics, utilities, and other support services.

Special Economic Zones (SEZs): Incentives and tax benefits for companies operating within SEZs engaged in semiconductor and electronics manufacturing.

7. Policy Framework and Support

Single Window Clearance: Streamlined processes for faster approval and clearances for setting up semiconductor facilities.

Legal and Regulatory Support: Ensuring a conducive legal and regulatory environment to protect intellectual property and ease doing business.

These initiatives collectively aim to create a robust semiconductor ecosystem in India, reducing reliance on imports, fostering innovation, and enhancing the country's global competitiveness in the technology sector.

The impact of the microchip industry on Indian government support for manufacturing microchips in India can be understood through several key aspects:

1. Economic and Strategic Importance

Microchips are crucial for modern technology, from smartphones and computers to automotive systems and home appliances. Recognizing the strategic and economic importance of this sector, the Indian government has prioritized boosting domestic microchip production to reduce dependence on imports and strengthen national security.

2. Government Initiatives and Policies

In recent years, the Indian government has introduced various initiatives to support and develop the microchip industry:

National Policy on Electronics (NPE) 2019: This policy aims to promote the growth of the electronics and semiconductor industry by providing incentives for manufacturing, research and development, and investment.

Production-Linked Incentive (PLI) Scheme: The PLI scheme offers financial incentives to manufacturers based on the value of their production. It aims to attract global semiconductor manufacturers to set up production facilities in India and boost local manufacturing.

Semiconductor Mission: Launched in December 2021, the Semiconductor Mission is a comprehensive strategy to support the development of semiconductor manufacturing and design capabilities in India. It includes setting up semiconductor fabrication units, design and innovation centres, and promoting research and development.

3. Investment and Infrastructure Development

To support the microchip industry, the Indian government has invested in developing infrastructure and creating an ecosystem conducive to semiconductor manufacturing:

Development of Semiconductor Fabrication Facilities: The government has planned to set up semiconductor fabrication units in India, attracting global players to invest in setting up plants. This includes support for building cleanroom facilities, supply chain development, and workforce training.

Research and Development: Significant investments are being made in R&D to advance semiconductor technology and innovation. This includes support for research institutions and collaborations with international tech companies.

4. Challenges and Solutions

While the Indian government has made significant strides in supporting the microchip industry, there are challenges:

High Capital Investment: Semiconductor manufacturing requires substantial capital investment. The government is working to address this by offering financial incentives and facilitating private sector investments.

Skill Development: The semiconductor industry requires a highly skilled workforce. The government is investing in education and training programs to build a talent pool in areas like semiconductor design and fabrication.

Supply Chain Dependence: India's semiconductor industry relies on a complex global supply chain for raw materials and equipment. Efforts are being made to establish more local suppliers and reduce dependency.

5. Impact on the Indian Economy

The growth of the microchip industry is expected to have a positive impact on the Indian economy:

Job Creation: Establishing semiconductor manufacturing facilities and R&D centres creates high-skilled jobs and contributes to economic growth.

Technological Advancement: A robust microchip industry supports technological innovation and development in various sectors, including electronics, telecommunications, and automotive industries.

Trade Balance: By increasing domestic production, India can reduce its import bill for semiconductors, positively impacting the trade balance.

Overall, the Indian government's support for the microchip industry is aimed at positioning India as a global player in semiconductor manufacturing, fostering technological advancements, and strengthening the economy.

Chapter: 5
Indian Microchip Manufacturing Industry

As of 2024, the Indian microchip manufacturing industry is evolving rapidly, driven by government initiatives, growing domestic demand, and global geopolitical shifts. Here's a detailed overview of the current landscape:

1. Government Policies and Support

A. National Policy on Electronics (NPE) 2019: The NPE aims to establish India as a global hub for electronics production, including semiconductors. It outlines strategies for increasing domestic manufacturing, reducing import dependency, and fostering innovation.

B. Production-Linked Incentive (PLI) Scheme: This scheme offers financial incentives to semiconductor manufacturers based on their production value. It is designed to attract international companies to set up production facilities in India and incentivize local manufacturing.

C. Semiconductor Mission: Launched in December 2021, this mission focuses on building a robust semiconductor ecosystem in India. It includes support for establishing semiconductor fabrication units, design centres, and R&D facilities.

2. Investment and Development

A. Semiconductor Fabrication Plants: The Indian government is actively working to attract investments for setting up semiconductor fabrication plants. Major international companies like TSMC (Taiwan Semiconductor Manufacturing Company) and Intel have shown interest, and the government is offering various incentives to facilitate these investments.

B. Research and Development Centres: India is also focusing on developing R&D centers to advance semiconductor technology and innovation. Institutions like the Indian Institute of Technology (IIT) and the Indian Institute of Science (IISc) are involved in semiconductor research, supported by government funding and collaborations with global tech firms.

3. Key Players and Investments

A. Domestic Companies: Companies such as Bharat Electronics Limited (BEL) and the Electronics Corporation of India Limited (ECIL) are involved in semiconductor and microchip production. However, they primarily focus on niche applications and components rather than large-scale chip manufacturing.

B. International Collaborations: Global semiconductor giants like Intel, TSMC, and GlobalFoundries are exploring opportunities in India. Intel has announced plans to invest in semiconductor research and manufacturing in India, reflecting the country's growing appeal as a manufacturing hub.

C. Startups and Innovation: India has a burgeoning ecosystem of semiconductor startups working on innovative solutions and technologies. These startups are contributing to advancements in semiconductor design, manufacturing, and applications.

4. Infrastructure and Supply Chain

A. Infrastructure Development: India is investing in developing the necessary infrastructure for semiconductor manufacturing, including cleanroom facilities and specialized equipment. Efforts are being made to build semiconductor manufacturing clusters and technology parks.

B. Supply Chain Challenges: The semiconductor supply chain in India is still developing. Challenges include dependency on imports for raw materials and equipment, as well as the need for more local suppliers. The government and industry stakeholders are working to address these issues by promoting local sourcing and enhancing supply chain resilience.

5. Challenges and Opportunities

A. High Capital Requirements: Semiconductor manufacturing requires significant capital investment, which poses a challenge for new entrants. The government's incentives and support mechanisms aim to mitigate this challenge.

B. Skill Development: There is a need for a skilled workforce in semiconductor design and manufacturing. The government and educational institutions are investing in training programs to build expertise in these areas.

C. Global Competition: India faces competition from established semiconductor hubs like Taiwan, South Korea, and China. However, India's growing market, strategic location, and supportive policies provide opportunities for significant growth.

6. Future Prospects

The future of the Indian microchip manufacturing industry looks promising, with several factors contributing to its growth:

Increasing Domestic Demand: As technology adoption increases across sectors like consumer electronics, automotive, and telecommunications, domestic demand for microchips is expected to rise.

Geopolitical Shifts: The ongoing geopolitical tensions and supply chain disruptions are prompting global companies to diversify their manufacturing bases, creating opportunities for India.

Technological Advancements: Continued investment in R&D and innovation will help India advance in semiconductor technology and attract further investments.

In summary, the Indian microchip manufacturing industry is in a growth phase, driven by supportive government policies, increasing investments, and a focus on developing infrastructure and skills. While challenges remain, the sector is poised for significant development in the coming years.

The Indian microchip industry is diverse, with a range of key players spanning both domestic and international firms. Here's a detailed look at the key players and their market shares:

1. Domestic Players

A. Bharat Electronics Limited (BEL):

Overview: A state-owned enterprise specializing in electronics and defense systems, BEL produces various semiconductor components and microchips.

Market Share: BEL has a niche position in the market, focusing primarily on defense and industrial applications.

B. Electronics Corporation of India Limited (ECIL):

Overview: Another state-owned company, ECIL, manufactures a range of electronic products, including semiconductor devices.

Market Share: ECIL is well-regarded for its contributions to the electronics and telecommunications sectors.

C. Micron Technology (India) Pvt Ltd:

Overview: A subsidiary of the global semiconductor company Micron Technology, this unit is involved in R&D and provides memory and storage solutions.

Market Share: While a subsidiary, Micron's presence contributes significantly to the domestic market due to its global expertise.

D. SABRE Semiconductor:

Overview: An Indian semiconductor company specializing in power management ICs and analog devices.

Market Share: SABRE holds a smaller yet significant share in the power management segment.

2. International Players with Significant Presence in India

A. Intel Corporation:

Overview: Intel is a leading global semiconductor manufacturer with a significant presence in India, focusing on R&D and technological innovation.

Market Share: Intel has a substantial market share in the high-performance computing and server segments. It is investing in local manufacturing and R&D facilities.

B. Texas Instruments (TI):

Overview: TI operates extensive manufacturing and R&D facilities in India, providing analog and embedded processing solutions.

Market Share: TI has a notable share in the analog and embedded market segments, leveraging its global reputation and local capabilities.

C. Qualcomm Inc.

Overview: Qualcomm is a key player in mobile and wireless technologies, with substantial operations in India, including R&D and support functions.

Market Share: Qualcomm holds a significant share in the mobile semiconductor market, especially in mobile processors and connectivity solutions.

D. GlobalFoundries

Overview: A major semiconductor foundry company with interest in expanding its footprint in India, particularly in fabrication and manufacturing.

Market Share: GlobalFoundries aims to capture a portion of the market through partnerships and investments in semiconductor manufacturing.

E. Broadcom Inc

Overview: Broadcom is involved in various semiconductor solutions, including networking and broadband, with a presence in India through its operations and partnerships.

Market Share: Broadcom holds a significant share in the networking and broadband segments.

3. Emerging and Niche Players

A. InnoMax Technologies

Overview: Specializes in semiconductor testing and assembly services, supporting the broader semiconductor ecosystem.

Market Share: InnoMax focuses on niche segments like testing and packaging, contributing to the overall market.

B. STMicroelectronics

Overview: A global semiconductor leader with operations in India, providing a range of semiconductor solutions including sensors and microcontrollers.

Market Share: STMicroelectronics: ST Microelectronics has a notable presence in various semiconductor segments.

4. Market Shares and Trends

Domestic Market Share: Domestic players, while influential, hold a smaller market share compared to international giants. The focus of domestic companies is often on niche markets and specialized applications.

International Market Share: International companies dominate the Indian semiconductor market due to their advanced technology, global expertise, and substantial investments in local operations. Companies like Intel, TI, and Qualcomm have significant shares in their respective segments.

5. Recent Developments

Increased Investment: There has been a rise in foreign direct investment (FDI) from global semiconductor companies setting up R&D and manufacturing facilities in India, which is expected to increase their market share.

Government Support: Initiatives like the PLI scheme and Semiconductor Mission are attracting both domestic and international players, which could shift market dynamics and increase the market share of companies investing in India.

6. Future Outlook

Growth Prospects: The market share of domestic players is expected to grow as new players enter the industry and existing players expand their operations. International players are likely to maintain a significant share due to their established presence and ongoing investments.

Technological Advancements: Advances in technology and the expansion of the semiconductor ecosystem will influence market shares and dynamics in the coming years.

In summary, the Indian microchip industry is characterized by a mix of domestic and international players, with international companies holding a significant market share due to their advanced technology and investments. The market is evolving with increasing domestic involvement and substantial foreign investments, shaping a dynamic and competitive landscape.

Chapter: 06

Challenges and Opportunities

The Indian microchip industry is poised for growth but faces several challenges and opportunities related to infrastructure and talent.

Challenges

1. Infrastructure Limitations

Fabrication Facilities: India currently lacks advanced semiconductor fabrication plants (fabs), which are crucial for producing high-performance microchips. Most fabrication is concentrated in regions like Taiwan and South Korea.

Supply Chain Issues: There is a dependence on global supply chains for raw materials and advanced equipment. Disruptions in these supply chains can impact production.

Research and Development (R&D): Limited investment in R&D infrastructure hampers innovation and the ability to keep pace with global advancements.

2. Talent Shortage

Skill Gap: There is a shortage of skilled professionals with expertise in semiconductor design, manufacturing, and testing. The industry requires specialized knowledge in areas such as VLSI design, semiconductor physics, and material science.

Educational Institutions: Although there are engineering colleges and technical institutes, the curriculum often lacks depth in semiconductor technologies. Many students graduate without hands-on experience in cutting-edge semiconductor design and fabrication.

3. Regulatory and Policy Challenges

Policy Uncertainty: Inconsistent and unclear policies regarding investment incentives, trade regulations, and intellectual property rights can deter investment.

Import Dependencies: Heavy reliance on imports for advanced semiconductor technology and equipment can affect the industry's growth and self-sufficiency.

4. Investment and Funding

High Capital Requirements: Establishing semiconductor fabs and R&D centres requires significant capital investment. Securing such funding can be challenging.

Investment in Startups: While there are numerous startups in the semiconductor domain, they often struggle to secure the necessary funding and support to scale their operations.

Opportunities

1. Government Initiatives

Policy Support: The Indian government has launched initiatives like the National Policy on Electronics and the Production Linked Incentive (PLI) scheme to boost the semiconductor industry. These policies aim to attract investment, build infrastructure, and promote local manufacturing.

Strategic Investments: There are plans to establish semiconductor manufacturing and design facilities in India, which can help reduce reliance on imports and create a more self-sufficient ecosystem.

2. Growing Market Demand

Consumer Electronics: With increasing demand for consumer electronics, smartphones, and IoT devices, there is a growing market for microchips. This trend can drive domestic production and innovation.

Automotive Sector: The rise of electric vehicles and smart automotive technologies presents new opportunities for semiconductor applications.

3. Talent Development

Educational Reforms: There is an opportunity to enhance curricula and training programs to better align with industry needs. Collaborations between academia and industry can provide practical training and research opportunities.

Skill Development Programs: Government and private sector initiatives can focus on upskilling professionals in semiconductor technologies through workshops, certifications, and industry-academia partnerships.

4. Global Partnerships

Collaborations: Partnerships with global semiconductor companies can bring in expertise, technology transfer, and investment. This can help India build a robust semiconductor ecosystem.

Export Opportunities: As domestic capabilities grow, India can become a significant player in the global semiconductor supply chain, exporting chips and related technologies.

Overall, while the Indian microchip industry faces significant challenges, there are also substantial opportunities for growth and development. Addressing infrastructure and talent issues, coupled with supportive policies and strategic investments, can pave the way for a thriving semiconductor industry in India.

The Indian microchip industry is undergoing significant transformation and presents numerous opportunities and trends. Here are some key aspects:

1. Government Initiatives and Policies

Atmanirbhar Bharat (Self-Reliant India) Initiative: The Indian government is pushing for greater self-reliance in microchip production. This includes policies aimed at reducing dependence on foreign chip manufacturers and fostering domestic production.

PLI Scheme for Electronics Manufacturing: The Production Linked Incentive (PLI) scheme offers financial incentives to boost domestic manufacturing of electronic components, including microchips. This aims to attract investments and increase local production capacity.

2. Investment and Infrastructure Development

Semiconductor Fabrication Facilities: There is a growing interest in establishing semiconductor fabs in India. Companies and governments are exploring partnerships and investments to set up fabrication plants, which could significantly boost local production.

R&D Investments: Investments in research and development are increasing, with both public and private sectors focusing on developing advanced chip technologies.

3. Growing Demand Across Sectors

Consumer Electronics: The rise in consumer electronics, including smartphones, tablets, and wearables, is driving demand for microchips.

Automotive Industry: The shift towards electric vehicles (EVs) and smart automotive technologies is creating new opportunities for microchip applications.

IoT and AI: The Internet of Things (IoT) and artificial intelligence (AI) are expanding, requiring advanced microchips for enhanced connectivity and processing power.

4. Global Supply Chain Shifts

Diversification of Supply Chains: The global semiconductor supply chain is experiencing shifts due to geopolitical tensions and supply chain disruptions. India is positioning itself as an alternative source of microchips, which could attract global companies looking to diversify their supply chains.

5. Talent and Skill Development

Educational Initiatives: Increased focus on semiconductor education and training programs is helping to build a skilled workforce capable of supporting the industry's growth.

Collaboration with Global Institutions: Partnerships with international institutions and universities are fostering knowledge exchange and skill development in semiconductor technologies.

6. Innovation and Startups

Emerging Startups: Indian startups are innovating in semiconductor design and manufacturing, contributing to the industry's growth. These startups are focusing on niche areas like specialized chips for AI and IoT applications.

Innovation Hubs: Establishing innovation hubs and technology parks is encouraging research and development in microchip technology.

7. Sustainability and Green Technology

Eco-Friendly Manufacturing: There is a growing emphasis on developing environmentally friendly manufacturing processes and sustainable chip technologies.

8. International Collaboration

Global Partnerships: Collaborations with international semiconductor companies and research institutions are enhancing India's capabilities in microchip design and production.

Overall, the Indian microchip industry is set to experience substantial growth driven by government support, increasing demand, and advancements in technology. As the sector matures, it holds the potential to become a significant player in the global semiconductor market.

India's journey in the semiconductor and microchip manufacturing industry, while relatively nascent compared to global leaders, has seen several noteworthy success stories and case studies. These examples illustrate India's growing capabilities and the potential for significant contributions to the global semiconductor supply chain.

Success Stories and Case Studies

1. Semiconductor Laboratory (SCL)

The Semiconductor Laboratory, based in Chandigarh, has been a significant player in India's semiconductor landscape. Originally established as a government entity, it has focused on research, development, and production of semiconductor devices. Although not a commercial fab, SCL's work in developing indigenous semiconductor technology has been crucial for strategic applications, particularly in space and defense.

Key Contributions: SCL has developed various application-specific integrated circuits (ASICs) and other semiconductor components critical for Indian space missions and defense equipment.

Impact: By focusing on high-reliability components, SCL has helped reduce India's dependence on imported technologies for critical applications.

2. Bharat Electronics Limited (BEL)

Bharat Electronics Limited, a state-owned company, has played a pivotal role in the Indian semiconductor industry, particularly in the defense sector. BEL has developed and manufactured a range of electronic components and systems, including microchips for defense and aerospace applications.

Key Contributions: BEL's semiconductor division has worked on developing critical components for radar systems, communication equipment, and electronic warfare systems.

Impact: BEL's initiatives have bolstered India's self-reliance in defense technology, providing secure and indigenous options for critical systems.

3. Reliance Jio and Altiostar

Reliance Jio, a major telecommunications company in India, partnered with Altiostar, a company specializing in open virtualized Radio Access Network (vRAN) technology. This collaboration focused on developing indigenous 5G network infrastructure, including the design and potential manufacturing of semiconductor components required for 5G technology.

Key Contributions: The partnership aimed at building a complete end-to-end 5G ecosystem in India, leveraging local manufacturing and design capabilities.

Impact: This initiative aligns with India's broader goals of digital sovereignty and technological self-reliance, particularly in critical and emerging technologies like 5G.

4. ISRO and Semiconductor Chips for Space Missions

The Indian Space Research Organisation (ISRO) has been a significant consumer of domestically produced semiconductor chips, particularly those developed by entities like SCL and BEL. ISRO has used these chips in various satellite missions, showcasing the reliability and quality of Indian semiconductor manufacturing.

Key Contributions: Development of radiation-hardened chips for use in space, capable of withstanding extreme conditions.

Impact: Demonstrates India's capability to produce high-specification semiconductors, crucial for space exploration and satellite technology.

5. Startups and Emerging Players

India has seen a rise in startups and smaller companies focusing on semiconductor design and innovation. Companies like Saankhya Labs and Signal chip have made strides in developing indigenous chipsets for communication technologies.

Saankhya Labs: Known for developing India's first indigenous chipset for software-defined radios, used in communication networks.

Signal chip: Developed indigenous semiconductor chips for 4G/LTE and 5G communications, reducing dependency on foreign suppliers.

Impact: These startups contribute to building a robust local ecosystem, focusing on innovation and specialized applications. They also exemplify the growing entrepreneurial spirit within the Indian semiconductor industry.

Lessons and Opportunities

Government Support: Many of these success stories have been supported by government initiatives, highlighting the importance of policy support in fostering the semiconductor industry.

Focus on Strategic Sectors: India has prioritized semiconductor development in strategic sectors like defense and space, which not only ensures national security but also builds expertise in high-reliability applications.

Indigenous Innovation: The growing number of startups and collaborations emphasizes the potential for indigenous innovation in semiconductors, which can be a foundation for broader industry growth.

Global Partnerships: Leveraging global partnerships for technology transfer and knowledge exchange has been a crucial strategy, enabling Indian companies to quickly scale up their capabilities.

While these success stories illustrate significant progress, the Indian semiconductor industry still faces challenges related to infrastructure, talent, and scale. However, with continued focus and investment, India has the potential to become a key player in the global semiconductor market.

Chapter: 7

Existing Microchip Manufacturing Units

As of now, India has a limited number of operational microchip manufacturing units, known as semiconductor fabrication plants or fabs. The country's semiconductor industry is still in its early stages, with most activities concentrated in design and testing rather than full-scale manufacturing. Here are some notable existing units and key players in the Indian semiconductor manufacturing landscape:

1. Semiconductor Laboratory (SCL), Chandigarh

Ownership: Government of India, Department of Space.

Focus: SCL focuses on research and development, and limited-scale manufacturing of semiconductor devices, including ASICs and MEMS devices, primarily for space and defense applications.

Capabilities: The facility has clean rooms and equipment for semiconductor processing, packaging, and testing. It is equipped for fabricating wafers up to 6 inches in diameter, though not on a commercial scale like leading global fabs.

2. SITAR (Society for Integrated Circuit Technology and Applied Research), Bangalore

Ownership: Government of India, under the Ministry of Defence.

Focus: SITAR specializes in the development of semiconductor devices for strategic applications in defense and aerospace sectors.

Capabilities: SITAR has facilities for developing silicon devices, focusing on small-scale, high-reliability production runs, and specialized applications.

3. SCL-ISRO Partnership

Focus: This collaboration leverages the Semiconductor Laboratory's facilities for developing high-reliability semiconductor components used in ISRO's space missions.

Capabilities: This partnership focuses on producing radiation-hardened chips and other components necessary for space applications.

4. BEL (Bharat Electronics Limited), Bangalore

Ownership: Government of India, Ministry of Defence.

Focus: BEL is primarily involved in producing electronic components and systems for defense applications, including some semiconductor manufacturing.

Capabilities: BEL has capabilities in semiconductor design and limited manufacturing, focusing on components used in radar systems, communications, and electronic warfare.

5. Hindustan Semiconductor Manufacturing Corporation (HSMC)

Status: As of the latest updates, HSMC's planned semiconductor fab had faced delays and challenges, including financial and partnership issues. The project aimed to establish a modern fab in India, but it has yet to come to fruition.

6. New Initiatives and Planned Fabs

Vedanta-Foxconn JV: A recent development involves Vedanta and Foxconn partnering to set up a semiconductor manufacturing facility in India. This project is part of India's broader strategy to boost its semiconductor manufacturing capabilities and reduce dependence on imports.

ISMC Analog Fab: Another significant proposal is from ISMC, which plans to set up an analog fab in India, focusing on producing analog chips and other components.

Challenges and Future Prospects

Infrastructure: Building and operating fabs requires advanced infrastructure, including clean rooms, sophisticated machinery, and stable power and water supplies.

Investment: Semiconductor manufacturing is capital-intensive, with initial setup costs for fabs running into billions of dollars.

Talent and Expertise: Developing a skilled workforce with expertise in semiconductor manufacturing is crucial. This includes engineers specializing in VLSI design, semiconductor physics, and manufacturing processes.

Government Initiatives: The Indian government has introduced various policies and incentives, like the Production Linked Incentive (PLI) scheme, to attract investment in semiconductor manufacturing.

India's existing microchip manufacturing units are foundational, and the country is actively seeking to expand its semiconductor ecosystem. The focus is on attracting global players, encouraging domestic investments, and developing a skilled workforce to support the industry's growth.

The Indian microchip industry has been evolving, and several lessons and best practices have emerged from its development

Lessons Learned

1. Government Support is Crucial: The Indian government's initiatives like "Make in India" and "Digital India" have been vital in encouraging investment and development in the semiconductor sector. Policies that provide incentives, subsidies, and infrastructure support are critical for nurturing the industry.

2. Skilled Workforce and Education: A well-educated and skilled workforce is essential for the growth of the microchip industry. India has benefited from its strong engineering education system, which has produced a large pool of talent in electronics and semiconductor technologies.

3. Importance of R&D: Research and development are crucial for innovation and staying competitive in the global market. Indian firms have increasingly focused on R&D to develop cutting-edge technologies and solutions.

4. Global Collaboration and Partnerships: Collaborations with global technology companies and research institutions have helped Indian companies access advanced technologies and best practices, fostering growth and innovation.

5. Supply Chain Challenges: The industry has faced challenges related to supply chain logistics, including the availability of raw materials and components. Addressing these challenges through better supply chain management and diversification is essential.

6. Focus on Niche Markets: Indian companies have found success by focusing on niche markets where they can compete effectively, such as design services and specific types of semiconductor applications.

Best Practices

1. Investment in Infrastructure: Developing state-of-the-art manufacturing facilities and investing in technology upgrades are critical for maintaining competitiveness in the microchip industry.

2. Promoting Startups and Innovation: Encouraging the growth of startups through incubation centres, funding, and mentorship can lead to innovation and new business models in the semiconductor sector.

3. Emphasizing Quality and Standards: Adherence to international quality standards and certifications ensures that Indian products are competitive globally. This includes focusing on processes like quality control, testing, and compliance.

4. Building Strong Ecosystems: Creating clusters or hubs that bring together different stakeholders, including manufacturers, suppliers, research institutions, and academia, fosters collaboration and innovation.

5. Sustainability and Environmental Responsibility: Emphasizing sustainable practices, such as reducing energy consumption and managing waste, is increasingly important in the semiconductor industry.

6. Continuous Learning and Adaptation: The industry is highly dynamic, requiring continuous learning and adaptation to new technologies, market trends, and regulatory changes. Training and development programs for employees are crucial.

By focusing on these lessons and best practices, the Indian microchip industry can continue to grow and become a significant player on the global stage.

Chapter: 8

Startups and Innovators

The Indian microchip industry, although still developing, has seen significant growth in recent years, driven by both startups and established players. Here are some notable startups and innovators in the Indian microchip industry:

1. Signal chip: Based in Bengaluru, Signal chip is known for developing India's first indigenous semiconductor chips for 4G and 5G NR modems. Their chips are aimed at telecom and networking applications.

2. Silexica: Originally a German company, Silexica has an Indian branch that focuses on developing software tools for optimizing multicore processing systems. This is crucial for the performance of microchips used in various applications, from automotive to telecommunications.

3. Saankhya Labs: Another Bengaluru-based company, Saankhya Labs specializes in designing software-defined radio (SDR) chipsets, which are used in a variety of applications including broadcast and broadband communication.

4. EInfo chips: A subsidiary of Arrow Electronics, eInfo chips provides semiconductor design services, including ASIC and FPGA design. They have worked on numerous projects involving microchips and embedded systems.

5. Ittiam Systems: This company focuses on multimedia processing solutions and has developed proprietary IP for video and image processing, which is integral to the functioning of microchips in multimedia devices.

6. HCL Technologies: While primarily known as an IT services giant, HCL has a semiconductor division that offers design and engineering services, including IP development, for microchips used in various industries.

7. CDAC (Centre for Development of Advanced Computing): Although not a startup, CDAC plays a pivotal role in the Indian semiconductor landscape, particularly in R&D for advanced computing technologies, including microchip design and development.

These companies and institutions are at the forefront of advancing India's capabilities in microchip design and manufacturing, contributing to the global semiconductor supply chain.

Startups and innovators have had a profound impact on the Indian microchip industry, contributing significantly to its growth and development. Here are some key impacts:

1. Indigenous Development of Technology

Startups like Signalchip and Saankhya Labs have developed indigenous semiconductor technology, reducing reliance on foreign technology and fostering self-reliance. Signalchip's development of India's first 4G and 5G modem chips is a prime example.

2. Innovation and Specialization

These companies focus on niche areas, driving innovation. For instance, Saankhya Labs specializes in software-defined radio chipsets, which can be used in various communication technologies, from broadcasting to broadband.

3. Boosting R&D Capabilities

Innovators are enhancing the research and development landscape in India. CDAC's role in advancing semiconductor technology showcases the importance of R&D in developing cutting-edge microchip solutions.

4. Employment and Skill Development

Startups in the microchip industry have created high-skilled jobs, attracted talent and promoted skill development. This, in turn, helps build a robust ecosystem of skilled professionals who can contribute to further advancements in the field.

5. Global Competitiveness

The presence of innovative startups has positioned India as a competitive player in the global semiconductor market. Companies like eInfochips, providing design services to global clients, illustrate India's growing influence in the industry.

6. Collaboration with Academia

Many startups collaborate with academic institutions for research, leading to a symbiotic relationship that promotes innovation and practical application of theoretical research.

7. Supply Chain Development

By creating demand for local manufacturing and ancillary services, these startups contribute to the development of a local supply chain for the semiconductor industry. This helps in reducing costs and improving the efficiency of production processes.

8. Government Support and Policy Influence

The success of these startups has also prompted the Indian government to introduce supportive policies and initiatives, such as the Production Linked Incentive (PLI) scheme for semiconductor manufacturing. This creates a favourable environment for further growth and investment in the industry.

9. Export Potential

Innovative products and solutions developed by these startups have the potential to be exported, contributing to India's export economy and positioning the country as a hub for semiconductor innovation.

10. Cross-Sectoral Impact

Microchips are fundamental to various sectors, including telecommunications, healthcare, automotive, and consumer electronics. The advancements made by Indian startups have cross-sectoral impacts, enhancing the technological capabilities and efficiencies of these industries.

In summary, startups and innovators are playing a crucial role in shaping the Indian microchip industry by driving technological advancements, creating high-skilled employment, fostering self-reliance, and positioning India as a competitive player in the global market.

Chapter: 9

Emerging Trends and Technologies

The future of the Indian microchip industry appears promising, driven by several factors including government initiatives, increasing demand for electronics, and advancements in technology. Here are some key prospects, emerging trends, and technologies likely to shape the industry's future:

Future Prospects

1. Government Initiatives and Support

The Indian government has introduced several initiatives to boost the semiconductor industry, such as the Production Linked Incentive (PLI) scheme, which aims to incentivize semiconductor manufacturing in India. This policy support is expected to attract investments and accelerate growth.

2. Growing Demand for Electronics

The rising demand for consumer electronics, smartphones, automotive electronics, and IoT devices is likely to drive the demand for semiconductors. India's large consumer market and increasing digitalization efforts will further fuel this demand.

3. Expansion of 5G and IoT

The rollout of 5G networks and the expansion of IoT ecosystems will require advanced semiconductor solutions, providing significant opportunities for growth in the Indian microchip industry.

4. Strategic Partnerships and Investments

Collaborations with global technology companies and investments in R&D are expected to enhance India's capabilities in semiconductor design and manufacturing. This includes potential joint ventures and partnerships that bring in expertise and technology.

5. Focus on Self-Reliance

India's push towards self-reliance (Atmanirbhar Bharat) in critical sectors, including semiconductors, is likely to encourage local production and reduce dependency on imports.

Emerging Trends and Technologies

1. AI and Machine Learning Integration

The integration of AI and machine learning into semiconductor design and manufacturing processes is emerging as a significant trend. This technology is used for optimizing chip performance, reducing design time, and enhancing manufacturing efficiencies.

2. Advanced Semiconductor Materials

The development and use of advanced materials, such as silicon carbide (SiC) and gallium nitride (GaN), are becoming more prevalent. These materials offer superior performance for high-power and high-frequency applications, which are critical for 5G and electric vehicles (EVs).

3. Chiplet Architecture

Chiplet architecture, which involves assembling multiple small chips (chiplets) into a single package, is gaining traction. This approach allows for greater flexibility, improved performance, and reduced costs compared to traditional monolithic chip designs.

4. Quantum Computing

While still in the early stages, quantum computing represents a future direction for the semiconductor industry. India has shown interest in developing quantum technologies, which could lead to innovations in quantum semiconductors.

5. Edge Computing

With the growth of IoT and real-time data processing needs, edge computing is becoming increasingly important. This trend is driving demand for specialized semiconductors that can process data locally at the "edge" of networks.

6. Automotive Semiconductors

The automotive industry's shift towards electric vehicles (EVs) and autonomous driving systems is spurring demand for specialized automotive semiconductors. These chips are crucial for battery management, power conversion, and sensor systems in vehicles.

7. RISC-V Architecture

The open-source RISC-V architecture is gaining popularity as an alternative to traditional architectures like ARM and x86. Its adoption could lead to new opportunities for Indian companies in designing custom processors.

8. Sustainability and Energy Efficiency

There is a growing focus on making semiconductors more energy-efficient and sustainable. This includes developing chips that consume less power and are produced using environmentally friendly processes.

The Indian microchip industry's future will be shaped by these trends and technologies, coupled with strategic policy support and increasing global integration. This combination positions India to become a significant player in the global semiconductor landscape.

India has significant potential to emerge as a global leader in the microchip industry, driven by a combination of market size, technological capabilities, and supportive government policies. To capitalize on these opportunities for growth and expansion, India can focus on several strategic areas:

1. Investment in R&D and Innovation

Increased Funding: Enhance investment in research and development (R&D) to foster innovation in microchip design and manufacturing. This includes both government funding and encouraging private sector participation.

Academic-Industry Collaboration: Strengthen collaborations between academic institutions and industry players to accelerate the translation of research into commercially viable technologies. Initiatives like establishing semiconductor research hubs can be crucial.

IP Development and Protection: Focus on developing indigenous intellectual property (IP) and ensure robust IP protection mechanisms to secure innovations.

2. Building a Skilled Workforce

Education and Training Programs: Develop specialized educational programs in semiconductor technology at universities and technical institutes. This includes curriculum updates and the introduction of practical training modules.

Skill Development Initiatives: Launch government-backed skill development programs aimed at training engineers and technicians in semiconductor fabrication, design, and testing.

Attracting Global Talent: Create incentives to attract global talent, including Indian professionals abroad, to contribute to the growth of the local semiconductor industry.

3. Infrastructure Development

Fabless Design Ecosystem: Support the growth of a fabless semiconductor design ecosystem, where companies design chips and outsource manufacturing. This model requires lower initial capital investment and can be a stepping stone toward establishing fabrication capabilities.

Foundry Development: Explore partnerships and joint ventures to establish semiconductor fabrication plants (fabs) in India. This requires significant investment but can be incentivized through subsidies, tax breaks, and streamlined regulatory processes.

Supply Chain Enhancement: Develop a robust supply chain for semiconductor materials, equipment, and components to support local manufacturing efforts.

4. Government Policy and Incentives

Incentive Schemes: Expand and refine incentive schemes like the Production Linked Incentive (PLI) program to attract more investment into the semiconductor sector.

Regulatory Support: Create a conducive regulatory environment that supports innovation and eases the process of setting up new businesses in the semiconductor industry.

Strategic Partnerships: Encourage and facilitate strategic partnerships with global semiconductor companies to bring advanced technology and manufacturing capabilities to India.

5. Focus on Emerging Technologies

Advanced Materials and Processes: Invest in research for advanced semiconductor materials (like silicon carbide and gallium nitride) and innovative manufacturing processes (such as EUV lithography).

Next-Generation Technologies: Develop capabilities in emerging areas like AI chips, quantum computing, and 5G/6G technologies, positioning India at the forefront of future technological advancements.

Sustainability Initiatives: Promote sustainable practices in semiconductor manufacturing, such as reducing water and energy consumption, to align with global environmental standards.

6. Market Expansion and Export Promotion

Global Market Integration: Strengthen trade relations and enter international markets, leveraging India's geopolitical position and market size.

Brand Building: Develop and promote a "Made in India" brand for semiconductors, emphasizing quality and innovation to build trust in global markets.

Local Market Development: Encourage the growth of local markets for semiconductors, particularly in sectors like consumer electronics, automotive, and telecommunications.

7. Strategic Alliances and International Cooperation

International Partnerships: Build strategic alliances with other countries and international organizations to share knowledge, access new markets, and gain technological know-how.

Bilateral and Multilateral Agreements: Engage in bilateral and multilateral agreements that facilitate technology transfer, joint ventures, and collaborative research.

By implementing these strategies, India can enhance its position in the global semiconductor value chain, achieve self-reliance, and potentially become a hub for semiconductor innovation and manufacturing in the coming years.

Chapter: 10

India's Potential for Global Leadership

To realize the potential of India's microchip manufacturing industry and establish it as a global leader, a concerted effort from all stakeholders—government, industry, academia, and the workforce—is essential. Here's a call to action for the key players involved:

1. Government

Policy and Regulatory Framework: Continue to enhance and streamline policies like the Production Linked Incentive (PLI) scheme to attract domestic and foreign investments in semiconductor manufacturing. Simplify regulatory processes to expedite project approvals and reduce bureaucratic delays.

Incentives and Subsidies: Provide financial incentives, such as tax breaks, subsidies, and grants, to encourage the establishment of semiconductor fabs and design houses. Support initiatives aimed at developing critical semiconductor infrastructure.

Public-Private Partnerships (PPP): Promote PPPs to facilitate investment in high-capital sectors like semiconductor fabs and R&D facilities. This includes encouraging global semiconductor giants to set up facilities in India in collaboration with local companies.

R&D Funding: Increase funding for research and development in advanced semiconductor technologies, including AI, quantum computing, and new materials. Establish centers of excellence and innovation hubs to foster cutting-edge research.

2. Industry Leaders and Entrepreneurs

Investment in Innovation: Prioritize investments in R&D to develop indigenous technologies and IP. Collaborate with academic institutions and global technology leaders to stay at the forefront of technological advancements.

Skill Development: Invest in training and upskilling the workforce to meet the demands of the semiconductor industry. This includes partnerships with educational institutions to ensure a steady supply of skilled engineers and technicians.

Sustainability: Adopt and promote sustainable manufacturing practices to reduce the environmental footprint of semiconductor production. This includes optimizing resource use and investing in clean technologies.

Collaboration and Networking: Engage in industry-wide collaborations and consortiums to share best practices, innovate, and address common challenges. Build networks to access global markets and supply chains.

3. Academia and Research Institutions

Curriculum Enhancement: Update curricula to include the latest developments in semiconductor technology, ensuring that graduates are industry-ready. Introduce specialized courses and programs focused on semiconductor design and manufacturing.

Research Collaboration: Work closely with industry partners on research projects that have practical applications. Encourage faculty and students to engage in cutting-edge research and participate in international conferences and workshops.

Incubation and Startups: Support the creation of startups through incubation centers and technology parks. Provide mentorship and resources to young entrepreneurs in the semiconductor space.

4. Workforce and Professionals

Continuous Learning: Embrace a culture of continuous learning and skill development. Stay updated with the latest trends and technologies in semiconductor manufacturing and design.

Innovation and Creativity: Encourage a mindset of innovation and creativity in solving industry challenges. Propose and experiment with new ideas and approaches that can drive the industry forward.

Networking and Community Engagement: Engage with professional networks and communities to share knowledge, collaborate on projects, and stay informed about industry developments.

5. Public Awareness and Support

Awareness Campaigns: Raise public awareness about the importance of the semiconductor industry for India's technological and economic future. Highlight success stories and the potential for job creation and innovation.

Support for Policies: Mobilize public support for government policies that promote semiconductor manufacturing and technology development.

6. International Community and Global Partners

Partnerships and Investments: Encourage global semiconductor companies to invest in India through joint ventures, technology transfers, and establishing manufacturing units.

Knowledge Sharing: Engage in knowledge-sharing initiatives to help Indian companies adopt best practices in semiconductor manufacturing and innovation.

This collective action plan aims to build a robust and competitive microchip manufacturing industry in India, capable of meeting both domestic and global demands. With coordinated efforts, India can establish itself as a key player in the global semiconductor landscape, driving technological advancement and economic growth.

Appendix A: Glossary of Microchip-Related Terms

1. ASIC (Application-Specific Integrated Circuit): A type of integrated circuit (IC) designed for a specific application or function rather than for general-purpose use.

2. Chiplet: A small, individual chip that can be combined with others to form a complete processor or system-on-chip (SoC). This modular approach allows for greater flexibility and efficiency in design and manufacturing.

3. Die: A small block of semiconductor material, typically silicon, on which a functional circuit is fabricated. A single wafer can contain multiple dies, each of which can function as an individual microchip.

4. Fab (Fabrication Facility): A manufacturing plant where semiconductor devices, such as microchips, are produced. Fabs are equipped with specialized machinery for processes like lithography, etching, and doping.

5. Fabless: A business model in which a company designs microchips but outsources the manufacturing to a separate semiconductor fabrication plant. This allows the company to focus on design and innovation without the high costs associated with maintaining a fab.

6. Foundry: A company or facility that manufactures semiconductors designed by other companies. Foundries provide the infrastructure and expertise for large-scale chip production.

7. FPGA (Field-Programmable Gate Array): An integrated circuit that can be programmed by the customer or designer after manufacturing. FPGAs are used in a variety of applications where flexibility and reconfigurability are required.

8. IP (Intellectual Property): In the context of semiconductors, IP refers to the proprietary designs and technologies used in microchip development. This can include circuit designs, manufacturing processes, and software tools.

9. Lithography: A process used in semiconductor manufacturing to transfer patterns onto a silicon wafer. This is a critical step in defining the structures and circuits on a chip.

10. Microcontroller: A compact integrated circuit designed to govern a specific operation in an embedded system. Microcontrollers typically include a processor, memory, and input/output peripherals.

11. Moore's Law: An observation made by Gordon Moore, co-founder of Intel, predicting that the number of transistors on a microchip would double approximately every two years, leading to increases in performance and decreases in cost.

12. Nano meter (nm): A unit of measurement equal to one billionth of a meter, commonly used to describe the size of features in semiconductor devices. Smaller nano meter processes typically lead to more efficient and powerful chips.

13. Photolithography: A specific type of lithography used in semiconductor manufacturing that employs light to transfer a geometric pattern from a photomask to a light-sensitive chemical photoresist on the substrate.

14. RISC (Reduced Instruction Set Computer): A CPU design strategy that uses a small, highly optimized set of instructions, as opposed to a complex set of instructions in complex instruction set computing (CISC).

15. RISC-V: An open standard instruction set architecture (ISA) based on the principles of RISC. RISC-V is free and open for anyone to use, promoting innovation and customization in processor design.

16. Semiconductor: A material with electrical conductivity between that of a conductor and an insulator. Semiconductors are the foundation of modern electronics, including microchips, transistors, and diodes.

17. SoC (System on Chip): An integrated circuit that incorporates all the components of a computer or other electronic system into a single chip. This can include the central processing unit (CPU), memory, input/output ports, and secondary storage.

18. Silicon Carbide (SiC): A semiconductor material known for its ability to handle high voltages and temperatures, making it ideal for power electronics and other high-performance applications.

19. Wafer: A thin slice of semiconductor material, typically silicon, used as the substrate for fabricating microchips. Wafers undergo various processes, including doping, etching, and deposition, to create integrated circuits.

20. Yield: The proportion of functional chips produced from a semiconductor wafer. Yield is a critical factor in determining the economic viability of chip production, as higher yields reduce costs.

Here is a list of notable microchip manufacturing units in India:

1. ISRO Semiconductor Laboratory (SCL)

Location: Chandigarh

Focus: Semiconductor technology development and fabrication for space and defense applications.

2. Bharat Electronics Limited (BEL)

Location: Bangalore, Karnataka

Focus: Defense electronics and semiconductor devices.

3. Semiconductor Complex Limited (SCL)

Location: Mohali, Punjab

Focus: Integrated circuit design and manufacturing.

4. Sahasra Electronics

Location: Noida, Uttar Pradesh

Focus: Semiconductor packaging and electronic manufacturing services.

5. CDIL (Continental Device India Ltd)

Location: New Delhi

Focus: Semiconductor devices, including diodes and transistors.

6. Analog Devices India

Location: Bangalore, Karnataka

Focus: Semiconductor and integrated circuit development.

7. Tata Consultancy Services (TCS)

Location: Various locations in India

Focus: Semiconductor and electronics research and development.

8. ASM Technologies

Location: Bangalore, Karnataka

Focus: Semiconductor engineering services and manufacturing.

This list includes some key players in the semiconductor and microchip manufacturing sector in India. The industry is evolving, and new units may emerge as the government and private sector continue to invest in this area.

Here's a timeline of key events in India's microchip industry

1980s: Early Developments

1984: The Government of India establishes the Department of Electronics (DoE) to promote electronics and semiconductor industries.

1990s: Initial Growth

1991: India begins liberalizing its economy, opening up opportunities for foreign investments in the semiconductor sector.

1994: The Semiconductor Complex Limited (SCL) in Mohali starts operations to support the growth of the domestic semiconductor industry.

2000s: Expansion and Investment

2000: Intel opens its first design centre in Bangalore, marking a significant entry of global semiconductor companies into India.

2004: The Semiconductor Association of India (SIA-India) is established to support the industry's growth and development.

2005: The Indian government introduces the National Policy on Electronics (NPE) to boost the electronics and semiconductor industry.

2010s: Growth and Innovation

2010: India sets up the National Electronics Mission to drive research and development in electronics and semiconductors.

2012: The Indian government launches the Electronics Development Fund (EDF) to support semiconductor and electronics innovation.

2014: The establishment of the Semiconductor Laboratory (SCL) in Chandigarh is reemphasized as a key institution for semiconductor R&D.

2020s: Significant Developments

2020: The Indian government announces a $1.4 billion incentive plan to attract semiconductor manufacturing investments under the Atmanirbhar Bharat (Self-Reliant India) initiative.

2021: Several global semiconductor firms, including Taiwan Semiconductor Manufacturing Company (TSMC) and GlobalFoundries, explore partnerships with Indian firms for local chip production.

2022: India and the US sign an agreement to strengthen cooperation in semiconductor technology and supply chains.

This timeline highlights the key milestones and initiatives that have shaped India's microchip industry over the decades.

www.ingramcontent.com/pod-product-compliance
Lightning Source LLC
Chambersburg PA
CBHW071953210526
45479CB00003B/920